Arepa Cookbook

Discover a Delectable Array of Arepa Flavors- Spicy, Cheesy, and
Sweet Varieties for Every Palate, Spanning Zesty to Decadent Delights

Pamela Ahart

Table of Content

INTRODUCTION

Welcome to the tantalizing world of Arepas, where tradition meets innovation, and every bite celebrates Latin American culinary excellence. I'm Pamela Ahart, and I'm thrilled to be your guide on this mouthwatering journey through Arepas's rich and diverse flavors.

Arepa is more than just a corn cake; it's a cultural icon, a beloved street food, and a canvas for culinary creativity. Born from the heartlands of Venezuela and Colombia, Arepas have found their way into the hearts and kitchens of food enthusiasts worldwide. In this cookbook, we will explore the intricate art of crafting these golden, crispy, and satisfying corn cakes, transcending borders to bring you the best of this beloved Latin American staple.

The Arepa is a versatile canvas, and we'll paint it with a palette of flavors that range from the zesty and savory to the decadently sweet. You'll find within these pages a collection of meticulously crafted recipes that showcase the immense variety of Arepa fillings and toppings, each with its own unique story and taste. Whether you're a seasoned Arepa fan or a newcomer to this delectable world, there's something here for everyone.

Our journey begins with the essentials: mastering the art of creating the perfect Arepa base achieving that delightful crunch on the outside while maintaining a soft and fluffy interior. We'll delve into Arepas's history and cultural significance, paying homage to the traditional recipes passed down through generations. But we won't stop there—this cookbook is also about pushing boundaries, so you can expect innovative twists and fusion creations that will elevate your Arepa game to new heights.

Prepare to explore a wide spectrum of Arepa flavors, from the fiery and spicy, where chili peppers and spices take center stage, to the rich and cheesy, where gooey, melted goodness meets the corny embrace of the Arepa. And don't forget about the sweet side, where Arepas are transformed into delectable sweets that will fulfill your sweet craving in the most decadent way conceivable.

Each recipe in this book is a labor of love, meticulously crafted and tested to ensure your success in the kitchen. Whether you're planning a casual brunch, a family dinner, a festive gathering, or simply indulging in a culinary adventure, "Arepa Cookbook: Discover a Delectable Array of Arepa Flavors- Spicy, Cheesy, and Sweet Varieties for Every Palate, Spanning Zesty to Decadent Delights" has you covered.

So, grab your apron, sharpen your culinary skills, and embark on a journey that celebrates the heart and soul of Latin American cuisine through the medium of Arepas. Your kitchen is about to become a canvas of flavor, and these Arepa recipes are your palette. It's time to create, savor, and share the magic of Arepas with your loved ones.

Let's dive in and discover the irresistible world of Arepas together!

Buen provecho!

-Pamela Ahart

1. AREPAS RECIPE

Total Time: 30 Mins

Servings: 8

Ingredients

Arepas

- 2 cups of precooked cornmeal
- 2 tsp salt
- 2½ cups of warm water
- oil for pan frying

Filling ideas

- Carnitas or Chipotle Shredded Chicken
- Magic Green Sauce or other sauce
- black beans
- sweet potatoes, sliced into thin pieces and sautéed in olive oil and salt until softened
- red onions
- Cotija cheese

Instructions

1. **Combine your ingredients:** Combine the salt with the precooked cornmeal. Mix the water, whisk to eliminate any solids, and mix until well blended. Give the mixture five to ten minutes to rest.
2. **Form the Arepas**: Divide dough into 8 pieces using your hands. Form each portion into a ball and gently press it down to form a disk approximately one inch thick.
3. **Fry the Arepas:** In a big, heavy skillet, heat a thin layer of oil, approximately ¼ inch deep, over medium heat. Fry the Arepas for about 6 minutes on each side after adding them. The outside of the Arepas should be dry-fried without getting too brown. Then place on paper towels to cool and drain.
4. **Assemble:** Place your fillings into the cut-in-half Arepas!

2. VENEZUELAN-STYLE AREPAS RECIPE

Prep Time: 5 Mins

Cook Time: 25 Mins

Active Time: 25 Mins

Resting Time: 10 Mins

Total Time: 40 Mins

Servings: 4

Ingredients

- 1½ cups of masarepa
- 1 cup of water, plus more as necessary
- 1 tsp vegetable oil
- Kosher salt
- 2 tsp butter
- Fillings as desired

Directions

1. Preheat the oven to 325°F (160°C) and set the oven rack in the center. Mix masarepa, water, and vegetable oil in a medium bowl. Use your hands to mix the ingredients together until a dough form. Take a tiny bit and press it between your hands. If the edges split, work the dough with 1 tbsp of water at a time until it becomes smooth and elastic but not sticky. Add salt to taste, cover, and let the dough sit for five minutes.
2. Roll the dough into four equal pieces and form them into balls. Flatten each ball into a disk approximately 4 inches in diameter and ½-inch-thick, using a wooden cutting board or a conventional cutting board with a layer of plastic wrap on top.
3. In a 12-inch nonstick or cast-iron pan, melt butter over medium-low heat. Add the Arepas and cook, moving them about the pan and flipping them from time to time, for approximately 5 minutes, until the initial side is slightly browned and a dry crust form. Cook until a dry crust forms on the second side, about 5 minutes longer. Then move to a baking sheet and bake for 10 minutes more, until it's well cooked. Remove from oven, let aside for 5 minutes, then divide, fill, and serve.

3. EASY AREPAS RECIPE

Prep Time: 20 Mins

Cook Time: 30 Mins

Total Time: 50 Mins

Servings: 8

Ingredients

- 2½ cups of lukewarm water (100°F-110°F)
- 1 tsp salt
- 2 cups of pre-cooked yellow cornmeal
- ¼ cup of canola oil
- Filling suggestions: shredded cheese, black beans.

Instructions

1. Set the oven's temperature to 350°F. Set a wire rack inside a baking pan.
2. Mix the salt and water in a big bowl. Gradually mix the cornmeal into the water with your fingertips until a soft, wet dough forms. Cover and set aside for 10 minutes.
3. Next, divide dough into 8 equal pieces and shape each piece into a ball. Form each ball into a ½-inch patty between your palms.
4. Heat the oil in a big cast-iron pan over medium heat until it is hot. Place the patties in the skillet in batches and cook for about 4 minutes on each side or until golden brown. Move the patties around the skillet occasionally to ensure they don't stick. Place the patties onto the wire rack.
5. Cook for 15 minutes. Take out of the oven and let it to cool fully or reheat it. Cut in half gently, horizontally, with a serrated knife—stuff with black beans, shredded cheese, or anything you like.

Notes

1. Add a tbsp of water and stir until the dough becomes flexible if your Arepas dough seems too dry and crumbles when molded. Avoid adding too much water as this will make the Arepas thick.
2. The dough should be sticky but not moist. Add a pinch of cornmeal to the dough if it is too moist until the desired consistency is reached.
3. Give the Arepas a tap if you need to check whether you cooked them all the way through. They're done if they make a hollow sound.
4. You can slightly moisten your hands before rolling the dough if it adheres to them.

5. They'll continue to cook after being taken out of the oven. Allow to cool. It will be doughy in the middle if you cut them while still hot.

4. AREPAS DE QUESO RECIPE (CHEESE AREPAS)

Prep Time: 5 Mins

Cook Time: 6 Mins

Total Time: 11 Mins

Servings: 4

Ingredients

- 1 cup of pre-cooked white or yellow Arepa flour
- 1 cup of warm water
- ⅓ cup of grated white or mozzarella cheese
- 2 tbsp butter
- Pinch salt

Instructions

1. Mix well to combine the cornmeal, warm water, cheese, 1 tbsp butter, and salt. Give the mixture five minutes to stand.
2. Knead for 3 minutes, moistening your hands as you work.
3. Form the dough into four tiny balls. Each ball should be placed between two plastic bags and flattened to a ½ inch using a flat pot cover.
4. Melt the butter in a nonstick skillet set over medium heat. After placing the Arepas in the pan, fry them for about 3 minutes on each side, until a golden-brown crust develops.

Notes

1. Cooked Arepas may be kept in the freezer for up to 30 days, or they can be kept in the refrigerator for up to 5 days in a Ziplock bag.

5. AREPAS PLUS FILLING IDEAS

Prep Time: 10 Mins

Cook Time: 20 Mins

Total Time: 30 Mins

Servings: 6

Ingredients

- 2 cups of pre-cooked corn flour (masarepa)
- 1¾ - 2 cups of warm water
- 1 tsp salt

Instructions

1. To begin, add the salt and warm water to a big bowl. Then, progressively add the cooked corn flour (masarepa), stirring after each addition.
2. Make the dough cool enough to handle, then knead it gently for one minute. After that, let it rest for ten minutes. It should be wet but not sticky when done.
3. If the dough is too dry and readily breaks when molded, add a tiny quantity of water. Add additional flour if it's too moist; humidity, temperature, and flour brand may all influence this.
4. Divide the Arepa dough into 6 sections (approximately 110-120 grams each Arepa) and form each into a ball before flattening into ½- ¾-inch (1.5-2 cm) thick disks.
5. Use your moist fingertips to gently massage any minor cracks until they are smooth.
6. Swirl some oil into a large nonstick pan or well-seasoned cast-iron skillet and heat it over medium heat. Cook the Arepas, three at a time, for approximately five minutes on each side, until they are golden brown on both sides.
7. Bake the Arepas for 10 minutes at 360 °F/180 °C in the oven if you want them to be really crispy.
8. Lastly, let them cool for a few minutes before slicing each Arepa approximately ¾ of the way around to form a pocket (a serrated knife works best when the Arepas are held warm with a dish towel). Then, load each pocket with all of your favorite fillings. Enjoy!

6. EASY AREPAS

Prep Time: 5 Mins

Cook Time: 10 Mins

Total Time: 15 Mins

Servings: 2

Ingredients

- 200g harina
- 0.5tsp fine salt
- 240ml warm water

Instructions

1. Combine three ingredients in a bowl and stir to blend. Next, knead the dough with your hands until it's smooth and shapes it into a ball.
2. Cut or shatter the ball into four uniformly sized pieces.
3. Press each piece out to form a flat, 10cm wide, and approximately 1.5cm thick disk. Roll each piece into a cylinder. I form my on the countertop and press down with a flat dough scraper to get it nice and smooth on either side. I then even out the edges.
4. After that, heat 1 tbsp olive oil in a frying pan over medium heat. Add one or two Arepas, based on the available space, and fry until pleasantly browned, 5 minutes on each side.
5. To serve, cut them in half and fill with delicious toppings!

Notes

1. These taste best when they are warm and just cooked.

7. AREPAS RECIPE WITH BLACK BEANS AND SALSA VERDE

Total Time: 1 Hr

Servings: 6

Ingredients

Arepas

- 300g of cornmeal, fine
- 1 tsp sea salt, heaped
- 1 tbsp of olive oil

Black beans

- olive oil
- 1 tsp cumin seeds
- 1 bunch of roughly chopped large coriander
- 1 tsp smoked paprika
- 800g of black beans from 2 tins
- 1 finely chopped green chilli

Pickled red onions

- 1 halved and finely sliced red onion
- 1 lime, juiced
- 1 pinch of flaky sea salt

Salsa verde

- 150g of feta or a vegan substitute, plus additional for serving
- 1 bunch of small coriander, leaves picked, plus extra for serving
- 4 tbsp of olive oil
- 1 zested and juiced lime
- 1 green chilli

To serve

- 1 bunch of finely sliced small radishes
- 2 limes, juiced

Instructions

1. Place the red onion, lime juice, and sea salt in a small bowl. Using your hands, squish them together until they begin to take on a vibrant crimson hue. Set aside to pickle gently.

2. To make the dough, fill a bowl with the cornmeal, oil, sea salt, and 400–450 ml of boiling water. Let it sit for a minute or so so the cornmeal can soak up some of the water. Next, using your hands, gradually incorporate the dough until well blended. You want it to stick together like Play-Doh. It should not crumble. Give the dough a 5-minute rest or up to 30-minute rest if you have time.

3. To prepare the black beans, heat up a medium-sized frying pan with some olive oil. Once heated, add the paprika, coriander stems, and cumin seeds. Cook for one minute. After that, boil the black beans for ten minutes while adding the can's liquid. Remove from the fire and stir in the chopped green chili and coriander leaves.

4. To make the salsa verde, combine the remaining ingredients in a food processor along with 30g of feta and half of the coriander leaves. Process until the salsa has a rich green color and a hint of creaminess. Adjust seasoning to taste, then save for dishing.

5. Pull off golf ball-sized pieces of dough and shape 8cm by 1cm-thick patties (you should be able to make 10) when it has rested (it should clean the bowl and be simple to deal with). Then heat some oil in a big frying pan. Add the Arepas, cover, and cook over medium heat for 7 minutes on each side until they're golden brown on both sides. Put in a heated oven while you finish frying the remaining Arepas.

6. Add chopped green chili and coriander leaves to the black beans to finish. Serve the Arepas warm, split open, and top with a dollop of black beans, salsa, pickled red onions, radishes, a squeeze of lime juice, and a crumble of the leftover feta.

8. HOMEMADE AREPAS

Prep Time: 10 Mins

Cook Time: 20 Mins

Total Time: 30 Mins

Servings: 8

Ingredients

- 2½ cups of lukewarm water
- 1 tsp salt
- 2 cups of pre-cooked white cornmeal
- ¼ cup of vegetable oil, or as needed

Directions

1. In a medium bowl, combine salt and water; progressively incorporate cornmeal using your fingertips until a soft, moist, and malleable dough forms.
2. Shape dough into eight balls with a diameter of two inches each. Pat each ball to make an Arepa patty that is 3/8 inch thick.
3. Fry Arepas in batches in a large pan over medium heat till golden brown, 4–5 minutes each side. Place cooked Arepas on a platter lined with paper towels to drain till cool enough to handle.
4. Make a pita-like pocket by cutting each Arepa in half horizontally with a narrow-serrated knife.
5. Enjoy!

9. VENEZUELAN AREPAS

Prep Time: 15 Mins

Cook Time: 25 Mins

Resting Time: 10 Mins

Total Time: 50 Mins

Servings: 8

Ingredients

- 2 cups of warm water
- 1 tbsp oil
- 1 tsp salt
- 2 cups of masa Arepa

Instructions

1. Mix the water, oil, and salt in a big bowl. Stir to dissolve the salt.
2. Add the masa Arepa slowly, mixing each time you add it.
3. Cover bowl with a moist tea towel and let aside for 10 minutes. If the dough is too dry after resting, add 1 tbsp of water.
4. Separate the dough into six equal portions, approximately ½ inch in diameter, and form each portion into a disc.

To Grill Your Arepas

5. Preheat a cast iron griddle to medium-high heat. Add the Arepas to the griddle after lightly oiling it.
6. To seal the dough, cook the Arepas for three to five minutes on each side. Then, lower the heat to medium-low or medium and cook the Arepas for 8-10 minutes on each side until they are golden brown and faintly charred. Adjust the griddle's heat as needed. (The Arepas should sound partially hollow when tapped and have a small puff.)
7. Remove the Arepas from the pan and cool for 10 minutes on a wire rack.
8. Use a sharp knife to cut the Arepas in half almost entirely if you plan to fill them.
9. Stuff and serve warm!!

To Bake Your Arepas

10. Set the oven to 350°F.
11. Place the Arepas on a hot griddle and seal for three to five minutes on each side after brushing with oil.
12. After that, bake the Arepas for 18-20 minutes until they sound hollow when tapped and have slightly inflated.
13. Before slicing, allow the Arepas to cool for ten minutes.
14. Stuff and serve warm!!

To Fry Your Arepas

15. You will need to make 12 rounds if you intend to cook your Arepas. Roll them into ¼-inch-thick, smaller discs.)
16. Fill a big skillet with one inch of hot oil. (The ideal oil temperature is 370F.)
17. Fry the formed Arepas in heated oil for 10 minutes until they're golden.
18. Remove the fried Arepas from the hot oil and place them on a dish coated with paper towels to finish cooking.
19. Serve warm!

Notes

1. Cooked Arepas keep nicely for two to three days at room temperature in an airtight container. Store them in the refrigerator for up to five days if you plan to keep them longer.
2. For optimal texture, reheat them in an oven or toaster oven.

10. EGG-STUFFED AREPA

Prep Time: 10 Mins

Cook Time: 20 Mins

Total Time: 30 Mins

Servings: 8

Ingredients

- 2 cups of
- 1¼ tsp. salt
- Corn oil, for frying
- 8 eggs

Directions

1. Combine Masarepa and 1 tsp. salt in a medium-sized bowl. Pour in 2 ½ cups of heated water. Mix well and leave for five minutes. Knead dough with damp hands until it's smooth. Cut dough into nine equal pieces. Using the remaining dough, form 8 little balls and set aside to fill in any holes later. Press the balls to a thickness of ¼" using your palms or a press.
2. In the meantime, add oil to a heavy pot to a depth of 1½". Heat oil until a deep-fry thermometer reads 325°F. Add Arepas to the oil. Cook for approximately 5 minutes, until the Arepas puff; then, move to plates lined with paper towels to drain and cool.
3. Make a 2-inch cut on one side of the Arepa using a knife to make a pocket. Crack the egg into a tiny ramekin or espresso-sized cup. Slide the egg gently into the pocket. Seal split end with saved part of uncooked dough.
4. Heat the oil to 350 degrees. Add Arepas with egg to oil. Cook for about 5 minutes, or until light golden brown on both sides with soft-set yolks. Drain on paper towel-lined plates. Season with the remaining salt.

11. AREPAS WITH SPICY BLACK BEANS

Prep Time: 35 Mins

Total Time: 35 Mins

Servings: 4

Ingredients

- 1 cup of yellow masarepa (precooked cornmeal)
- 1 cup of warm water
- ½ tsp salt, divided
- 4 tbsp corn oil, divided
- 1 large diced poblano
- 1 small diced onion
- 1 minced garlic clove
- ¼ tsp ground cumin
- 1 (15 ounce) can rinsed no-salt-added black beans
- 1 (15 ounce) can no-salt-added diced tomatoes
- ¼ cup of chopped fresh cilantro, extra for garnish
- 2 tbsp lime juice, and lime wedges for serving
- ¼ cup of crumbled cotija cheese or queso fresco

Directions

1. In a medium bowl, mix masarepa, water, and ¼ tsp salt. Mix until a uniform dough is formed. Put away.
2. After that, add 1 tbsp oil to a large saucepan over medium-high heat. Add onion and poblano; cook, stirring occasionally, for 3-5 minutes, until it's softened. Add the garlic, cumin, and the remaining ¼ tsp salt. Cook, stirring, for approximately 30 seconds, until it's fragrant. Add beans and tomatoes and stir. Bring over high heat to a simmer. Decrease heat to maintain a simmer and continue to cook, stirring periodically, for 15-20 minutes, until the mixture has thickened. Take off the heat and mix in the lime juice and cilantro.
3. Next, divide dough into four equal balls and roll them into disks that are ½-inch-thick and 4 inches broad. Place a large pan over medium-high heat with 1 ½ tsp of oil. Add 2 of the Arepas and cook for 7-8 minutes, flipping once, until golden brown. Continue using the remaining 1 ½ tsp of dough and oil.
4. Place some of the bean mixture and cheese on top of the Arepas. If preferred, garnish with more cilantro and serve with lime wedges.

12. AREPAS RECIPE WITH FILLINGS IDEAS

Prep Time: 10 Mins

Cook Time: 10 Mins

Resting Time: 5 Mins

Total Time: 25 Mins

Servings: 2

Ingredients

- 10 garlic cloves
- 1 ¼ tsp kosher salt, divided
- ¼ tsp Mexican oregano, or regular dried oregano
- ¼ tsp ground ancho chile powder
- ⅛ tsp dried red pepper flakes
- 1 tsp olive oil
- 2 cups of Arepa corn meal made from precooked ground corn
- ½ cup of grated manchego cheese
- 2½ cups of hot water
- 1 tbsp extra-virgin olive oil

Instructions

1. Smash the garlic with the flat side of a chef's knife and transfer to a small bowl. Sprinkle with 1 tsp kosher salt and pulverize the garlic into a purée with a fork.
2. Stir in the olive oil, anchovies, oregano, and red pepper flakes. Make sure the spices and olive oil are fully incorporated into the garlic by continuing to massage the mixture.
3. Combine the cheese, flour, and the remaining ¼ tsp salt in a medium-sized bowl.
4. Add the hot garlic paste and stir it into the flour mixture with a fork or your fingertips. Add the boiling water all at once, stirring with a fork until a dough form.
5. The dough will get thicker as it cools down. This occurs swiftly. After putting the dough on a surface, knead it a few times until it becomes solid. When the dough solidifies, it shouldn't be sticky.
6. Cut the dough into four equal halves. Flatten each piece into a disk by rolling it between your palms.
   Tip: Flatten thick disks to a diameter of around three inches. Flatten to roughly 5 inches in diameter for thin disks like the ones shown.

7. Warm up a large amount of olive oil over medium-high heat in a grill or sauté pan so that it coats the top. Add the dough disks once the oil is heated. Bake for five minutes on each side, until the tops of the muffins resemble their surfaces.
8. Serve warm.

13. VENEZUELAN AREPAS RECIPE

Prep Time: 20 Mins

Cook Time: 15 Mins

Total Time: 35 Mins

Servings: 8 Arepas

Ingredients

- 1 red pepper, cut into thin slices
- 1 green pepper, cut into thin slices
- 1 small Spanish onion, cut into thin slices
- 2 chicken breasts without bone, cut in half lengthwise and thinly sliced
- 2 cups of white pre-cooked cornmeal
- 2¼ cups of water
- 1 tbsp of Adobo seasoning
- 2 tbsp of Worcestershire sauce
- 1 package of Queso Blanco sometimes called Queso Fresco, Queso Ranchero
- 2 tbsp vegetable oil or olive oil
- 1 tsp of salt and pepper
- 1-2 tbsp of Cholula hot sauce, depending on how much spice you like
- 4 tbsp of butter, optional

For Adobo Seasoning

- 1 tsp kosher salt
- 1 tsp fresh ground black pepper
- 1 tsp turmeric
- ¼ tsp dried oregano
- ¼ tsp garlic powder

Instructions

1. Set your oven's temperature to 300 degrees.
2. Combine the water, salt, and pepper in a big bowl and stir.
3. Next, gradually add your corn meal to the water and stir thoroughly. You're preparing the dough for your corn patties. It should be damp but not wet, much like clay. Simply add 1 tbsp extra water at a time until your corn meal mixture is wet if it gets too dry, which will happen on dryer days.
4. When the corn meal mixture is ready, take a big ball and roll it into a ball. Then, make it into a patty shape, making sure the sides are smooth, like making a hamburger. Have fun!
5. Repeat until you have made around 7-8 patties, or all of your corn meal.
6. Next, make the Arepas.
7. Pre-heat a large heavy-bottom pan with 1 tbsp vegetable oil on medium.
8. Add the corn patties (Arepas) to the pan when it's hot and cook for about 5 minutes on each side, or until a lovely crust form.
9. If some Arepas don't fit in the pan at once, you may have to cook them one at a time.
10. After they are done, transfer them to a large cookie sheet and return to the oven to continue cooking. It warms them inside and improves the crust. They won't burn, so you'll keep them in there until you're done preparing the remainder of your dinner.
11. While the Arepas are baking, heat another tbsp of vegetable oil in the same pan that was used to crisp them.
12. After that, add the peppers, onions, and garlic to the pan and cook for a few minutes.
13. After that, season your sliced chicken with Adobo, put it to the pan with the peppers and onions, and cook it until it is thoroughly cooked.
14. Put the chicken over low heat, add the Worcestershire and Cholula sauces, stir, and cover once the chicken is done.
15. Now, cut the Queso Blanco cheese into slices and arrange them on a platter.
16. Then, remove the Arepas from the oven and place them on a platter.
17. Finally, transfer the peppers and chicken to a bowl and set all of these items out on the table so that people can put their Arepas together.

Assembling the Arepas

18. Slice the Arepa open like a bun with a sharp knife (be cautious, it's hot!) and add some butter.
19. Melt a tiny piece of butter and mix it into the Arepa.
20. Add some cheese slices.
21. Add your mixture of meat and vegetables.
22. Put the Arepa's top back on.
23. ENJOY!! It is messy.

14. VEGAN AREPAS PLUS DELICIOUS AREPA FILLINGS

Prep Time: 3 Mins

Cook Time: 10 Mins

Resting Time: 5 Mins

Total Time: 18 Mins

Servings: 4

Ingredients

- 2 cups of cooked white maize flour corn meal
- 2½ cups of water
- 1 tsp fine salt

To serve

- Creamy Vegan Sauce
- Marinated Grilled Tofu

Optional

- 1 bunch arugula
- ½ sautéed red onion
- 1 pinch red chilly if you like to make it spicy

Instructions

1. Prepare the recipe for Marinated Grilled Tofu.
2. Prepare the Creamy Sauce for Everything in the Notes in 5 Minutes.
3. Add the salt, water, and precooked cornmeal and stir. In a bowl knead for two minutes, then give it five more minutes to rest.
4. Make four balls out of the dough and press each one down with your hands until it forms a three-inch disc. Press more on the edges and less on the souls of your palms as you shape the discs to resemble a flying saucer.
5. Grill them for five minutes on each side over medium heat.
6. Cut the red onions in the meantime, and sauté them in one tsp of cooking oil. You may also choose to add the residual marinade fluid from the grilled tofu (it should have some soy sauce, ginger, and garlic).
7. To make the Arepas, carefully cut one side off without going all the way through. Then, fill the Arepas with the sauce, the sautéed onions, the greens, and the tofu chunks.

Prep Time: 10 Mins

Cook Time: 40 Mins

Total Time: 50 Mins

Servings: 6

Ingredients

For the Shredded Chicken

- 1⅓ Pounds chicken breasts
- ½ medium chopped onion
- 1 cilantro sprig
- ½ tsp salt
- 4 cups of water, or to cover chicken
- 3 peeled and sliced avocados

For the Sauce

- 1 lime, juiced
- 1 medium diced onion
- 1 chopped cilantro sprig
- 2 tbsp mayonnaise or Greek yogurt
- ½ tsp salt
- 1 pinch black pepper

Directions

For the Shredded Chicken

1. In a large pan, combine the salt, water, onion, and cilantro sprig. Raise to a simmering medium. When the chicken is done, add it and simmer it slowly.
2. Shred the chicken with two forks or in a low-speed mixer. Set aside.

For the Sauce

3. Combine the lime juice, Greek yogurt or mayonnaise, salt, and pepper in a bowl. Put away.
4. Transfer the avocado slices (reserving a few for garnish) to a second, bigger bowl.
5. Add chopped onion to the bowl and taste.
6. Stir in avocado.

7. Add chopped cilantro to the bowl and stir.
8. Pour in the lime-yogurt or lime-mayonnaise dressing. Blend well. For texture, keep part of the avocado bits bigger, but you may adjust the amount of avocado to your preferred consistency.
9. Add one or two batches of the shredded chicken. Blend well. If necessary, taste and adjust the spices.
10. Your Arepa is ready for your reina pepiada. Add a few slices of avocado and a final sprinkling of lime and cilantro as garnish. Savor this lovely delight.

16. COLOMBIAN AREPAS

Total Time: 35 Mins

Servings: 4

Ingredients

- 1 cup of Arepa flour (precooked cornmeal)
- 1 cup of crumbled ricotta salata (¼ pound)
- 1 cup of water
- 2 tbsp water
- ⅛ tsp salt
- ¼ cup of vegetable oil

Directions

1. In a bowl, combine Arepa flour, cheese, and ⅛ tsp salt; whisk in water until well combined.
2. Let rest 1–2 minutes until water is absorbed to make a soft dough (dough will thicken).
3. Roll three level tbsp of dough into a single cylinder, then flatten it between your palms and press gingerly to form a patty that is ¼ inch thick and 2 ½ to 2 ¾ inches wide. To prevent cracks, lightly press the dough around the side. Transfer to a surface covered with wax paper.
4. Form more disks with remaining dough in the same manner, transferring to a wax-paper-lined surface.
5. In a large nonstick or cast-iron pan, heat oil over medium heat until it shimmers. Fry the Arepas in two batches, flipping once, for a total of eight to ten minutes each batch, until they're deep golden in spots.
6. Drain on paper towels.

17. COLOMBIAN-STYLE AREPAS RECIPE

Prep Time: 25 Mins

Total Time: 25 Mins

Servings: 4

Ingredients

- 1½ cups of masarepa (see notes)
- 2 ounces (about ½ cup) finely crumbled queso fresco (optional)
- 1 cup of water, plus more as necessary
- 1 tsp vegetable oil
- Kosher salt
- 2 tsp butter

Directions

1. In a medium-sized bowl, combine masarepa, cheese (if using), water, and vegetable oil. Knead the ingredients with your hands until it forms a dough. Take a tiny bit and press it between your hands. If the dough cracks along the edges, knead in additional water one tbsp at a time until the dough is smooth and elastic but not sticky. After adding salt to taste, cover the dough and leave it for five minutes.
2. Roll the dough into four equal pieces and form them into balls. Use a wooden cutting board or a regular cutting board with a plastic wrap or parchment paper on top to flatten each ball into a disk that is about 5 inches across and ¼ inch thick.
3. Melt butter in a 12-inch nonstick or cast-iron pan over medium-low heat. Add the Arepas and cook, moving them about the pan and flipping them from time to time, for approximately 5 minutes, until the initial side is somewhat browned and a dry crust form. After flipping the Arepas, heat for 5 minutes until a dry crust forms on the other side. Cook the Arepas for another 5 minutes or more, turning them over every minute or so, until they are largely dry and quite firm. Serve hot with your preferred toppings, cheese, or melted butter.

18. COLOMBIAN AREPA RECIPE

Prep Time: 20 Mins

Cook Time: 20 Mins

Total Time: 40 Mins

Servings: 2

Ingredients

- 1 cup of pre-cooked Arepa flour, white or yellow
- 1 cup of water warm
- 2 tbsp butter
- Salt to taste
- Cooking Spray

Instructions

1. Combine the butter, Arepa flour, water, and salt in a large bowl.
2. Combine all ingredients and knead until a soft consistency is achieved.
3. If it's too dry, add more water. If it's too wet, add more Arepa flour.
4. Form spheres of medium size and sandwich them between two plastic sheets.
5. Using a rolling pin, flatten the balls until the appropriate thickness is achieved. Most of them are ½ inch thick.
6. Make sure your Arepa is spherical; if necessary, trim off any excess to make it so.
7. Spray a griddle with cooking spray or similar and heat it to medium.
8. You may add the Arepas one by one once the griddle reaches the appropriate temperature.
9. Cook until the Arepas are brown on both sides or are toasted to your desired consistency.

19. COLOMBIAN AREPA CON QUESO RECIPE

Prep Time: 10 Mins

Cook Time: 15 Mins

Total Time: 25 Mins

Servings: 4

Ingredients

Arepa

- 1 cup of pre-cooked white or yellow Arepa flour
- 1 cup of warm water
- ½ cup of grated white or mozzarella cheese
- 2 tbsp butter
- pinch salt

Filling

- Mozzarella cheese or cheese of preference

Instructions

1. Mix well to combine the cornmeal, warm water, cheese, butter, and salt. Give the mix five minutes to sit.
2. Wet your hands as you work and mix for around 3 minutes until you have a soft dough.
3. Form the dough into four tiny balls. Each ball should be placed between two plastic bags and flattened to a ½ inch using a flat pot cover. Alternatively, you might flatten the dough balls into discs of uniform size.
4. Put butter in a nonstick pan on medium.
5. Cook the Arepas in a pan for approximately three minutes per side, until they are golden brown and a crust form.
6. Slice the Arepas open gently, then stuff them with cheese.
7. Return to the pan and simmer until the cheese melts.

20. AREPAS CON QUESO RECIPE

Prep Time: 20 Mins

Cook Time: 10 Mins

Total Time: 30 Mins

Servings: 16

Ingredients

- 4 cups of precooked white cornmeal
- 4 cups of shredded Mexican cheese blend, divided (or mozzarella cheese)
- 1 cup of crumbled cotija cheese
- 1 tsp coarse Kosher salt
- 3½ cups of warm water
- ¼ cup of melted unsalted butter

Instructions

1. Mix the cornmeal, slat, cotija cheese, and two cups of the shredded cheese in a big bowl.
2. To make a soft dough, add the water and melted butter. It ought to be like playdough you'd make at home.
3. Put a kitchen towel over the bowl and leave it alone for 10 minutes.
4. Make the dough smooth and soft by kneading it for a few minutes. It should stay in shape but be easy to work with.
5. Make sixteen equal balls out of the dough.
6. After that, roll each ball of dough into a ¼-inch-thick, 5-inch circular.
7. Put a few tbsp of the cheese that you have left over in the middle of the patty.
8. Place another piece of dough on top of it and squeeze the edges shut. Seal well.
9. Form the dough into a patty approximately 3 inches in width and ½ inch in thickness.
10. Repeat with the remaining dough balls. Put away.
11. Next, preheat an electric griddle to 325°F or a 12-inch cast iron pan to medium-high heat.
12. Once the pan is heated, put a tiny pad of butter over the whole surface of the skillet.
13. Place the Arepas in the pan and heat for 5 minutes, until they're crispy and golden.
14. Cook for five minutes on the other side after flipping.
15. Transfer to a wire rack to chill while you finish the remainder. Place in a heated oven.

21. ENCANTO-INSPIRED AREPAS CON QUESO WITH AVOCADO MASH

Prep Time: 10 Mins

Cook Time: 20 Mins

Total Time: 30 Mins

Servings: 4

Ingredients

Arepas

- 1 cup of pre-cooked white cornmeal
- 1 cup of water
- ½ tsp kosher salt
- 4 tbsp grated queso Blanco
- nonstick cooking spray, for greasing
- 2 tbsp unsalted butter, for serving

Avocado cilantro mash

- 2 small peeled, pitted, and cubed Hass avocados, ripe
- 1 lime, juiced
- ¼ tsp red pepper flakes
- ½ tsp kosher salt
- 2 tbsp finely chopped fresh cilantro

Instructions

1. **Make the Arepas:** Place the cornmeal in a bowl of suitable size. Pour in the water, then add the salt and blend with a rubber spatula. At first, the dough will appear rather moist, but as you mix, it will absorb the water.
2. Place the dough onto a sanitized surface and shape it into a log that is 8 inches long and 2 inches (5 cm) broad. Divide into four equal halves.
3. Form a 4-inch-wide disc from one portion of dough using the palm of your hand. Put one spoonful of queso Blanco in the center and cover with the dough by folding it over itself. Press the dough into a disc that is 4½ inches in diameter once again. If some cheese is visible, tamp it down with your fingers. Repeat with the cheese and leftover dough.

4. Preheat a big nonstick frying pan over high heat. Apply nonstick spray to the pan, add the Arepas, and cook, stirring occasionally, for 3½ to 4 minutes, until a crispy, golden brown crust develops. Turnover and continue cooking for an additional three to four minutes, until the other side is golden brown (some cheese may leak out and scorch, giving the Arepa a delightful texture).
5. Prepare the avocado-cilant mash in the interim: Mash the avocado with a fork after adding it to a medium-sized bowl along with the lime juice, red pepper flakes, and salt.
6. Drizzle the Arepas with butter and garnish with a pinch of cilantro and avocado mash.
7. Enjoy!

22. AUTHENTIC VENEZUELAN AREPAS RECIPE

Prep Time: 8 Mins

Cook Time: 12 Mins

Rest Time: 5 Mins

Total Time: 25 Mins

Servings: 4

Ingredients

- 1¼ cups of lukewarm water
- 1 pinch salt optional
- 1 cup of pre-cooked Harina, white or yellow Arepa flour

Instructions

1. Put water into a big bowl.
2. Add in salt until it dissolves.
3. Add in half of the Arepa flour.
4. Add in the remaining Arepa flour until well mixed.
5. Knead the dough until it is soft, flexible, and free of lumps.
6. Give the mixture five minutes to rest.
7. Pre-heat a budare, griddle, cast iron pan, or non-stick skillet on medium-high.
8. Separate the dough into six equal balls.
9. Make a flat, round patty with each ball using your hands. The standard size for an Arepa is that of an English muffin.

10. You can fix cracks in the Arepa sides by wetting your fingers and pressing them together.
11. Coat the griddle or budare with a thin coating of oil. To do this, a griddle should be lightly greased.
12. Cook the Arepas for five to six minutes on a griddle or grill pan.
13. Decrease the heat to medium, rotate the Arepas, and continue cooking for 5 minutes on the second side.

23. AUTHENTIC AREPAS RECIPE

Prep Time: 10 Mins

Cook Time: 10 Mins

Rest Time: 5 Mins

Total Time: 25 Mins

Servings: 10

Ingredients

- 600 ml lukewarm water
- 480 ml fine cornmeal
- 1 tbsp salt

Instructions

1. Combine salt and water in a bowl.
2. Scoop or scrape in the flour one little tbsp at a time.
3. When everything is mixed hold off on kneading for a few minutes.
4. After that, knead dough until it forms a smooth ball that doesn't stick to the bowl.
5. Form the dough into eight to ten balls, each of which you should flatten with your palm. Make 8-10 Arepas with a 10 cm diameter.
6. Warm a frying pan (or two, for speed) over medium-high heat. Cook until golden brown, about 5 minutes on each side.
7. Give the Arepas some time to cool. Assist. You may split them up and put any fillings you choose inside.

24. VENEZUELAN AREPAS

Prep Time: 20 Mins

Cook Time: 25 Mins

Total Time: 45 Mins

Servings: 8

Ingredients

- 2 cups of precooked corn meal
- 2 ½ cups of water, room temperature
- 1 tsp salt
- 1 tbsp vegetable oil

Directions

1. Preheat the oven to 410 degrees Fahrenheit.
2. Pour the water into a big bowl. Check that it is at room temperature.
3. Put the salt in. Mix it well with a mixer, a fork, or a spoon to make sure it breaks down well.
4. Add the corn meal gradually, a little at a time, while beating the mixture.
5. Mix the corn meal, water, and salt until they are completely dissolved after adding all of the flour.
6. Set aside the masa in its bowl. Then rest for 5 minutes to fully hydrate the flour. Since there is no gluten in this maize flour, the dough does not require kneading. Masa should be silky, yet flexible and firm.
7. Preheat your budare (or comal, griddle, cast-iron pan, or nonstick pan) over medium heat while you wait for the five minutes to pass. Coat with a little oil.
8. Wet your hands in a small dish of water before making the Arepas.
9. Get your hands wet and take about 2 tbsp of the masa. To make a small ball, the masa should be able to fit in your hand without much trouble.
10. Place the masa ball between your crossed palms, one on top of the other. Move your right hand in a circular motion while maintaining the spherical shape of the masa and pushing it into a flat disk.
11. Lastly, shape your Arepa by passing the masa disc quickly between your hands and pressing it softly until it reaches a thickness of ¾ inch and a width of 4 inches. To keep them as spherical and crack-free as possible, swiftly dip your hands into the water bowl and smooth the edges.

12. Transfer your Arepas in batches onto a nonstick pan or budare griddle that has been warmed. Allow to turn golden on all sides, 4 to 5 minutes per side. Check them frequently to ensure that they do not burn.
13. After that, place Arepas on a baking sheet and bake for 10 minutes, until well browned on both sides. Arepas should be puffy enough to sound like an empty box when softly tapped on top.
14. Serve Arepas hot, whether you load them with your preferred filling or serve them by themselves with your preferred guiso or stew from Venezuela.

25. COLOMBIAN CORN AND CHEESE AREPAS

Total Time: 1 Hr

Servings: 11 Large Arepas

Ingredients

- 3 cups (about 1 pound) of precooked white corn flour
- 2 tbsp sugar
- 5 tbsp melted unsalted butter
- 1½ pounds coarsely grated soft fresh cheese (about 4 cups, well packed)
- 8 ounces coarsely ground cow's-milk cheese (about 2 cups)
- 1½ tsp salt

Directions

1. Mix the flour and sugar in a big bowl. Mix in 3 cups of warm water gradually with your fingertips, then 4 tbsp butter. Work into a soft dough.
2. Knead in the cheese one cup at a time. If mixture appears dry, add another 1-2 tbsp of water. After tasting the dough (as certain cheeses are very salted), knead in ½ tsp salt at a time. Knead the dough until it is smooth and soft, without any lumps. Cover with a moist towel and leave to rest for at least fifteen minutes.
3. After that, preheat a grill or broiler to high heat. Cut the dough into eleven equal pieces, about 5 ounces or ½ cup of each. Form into balls with your hands and place on a tray with a moist kitchen towel on it. Press every ball into a thick, three-quarter-inch-diameter circle that is level on all sides. Place back on the tray and cover.

4. Cover the broiler or grill rack with aluminum foil and lightly apply the remaining tbsp of butter on the foil. Place the Arepas on foil and cook them 4 inches away from the heat source, rotating them once, for about 10 minutes on each side, until they are golden brown and speckled on both sides. Serve right away as an appetizer for soups or stews or for breakfast (like corn muffins).

26. CHEESE AREPAS RECIPE

Servings: 4

Ingredients

- 1 cup of white or yellow Arepa flour
- 1 cup of warm water
- ⅓ cup of grated mozzarella or white cheese
- 2 tbsp of butter
- Salt

Instructions

1. Mix corn flour, hot water, cheese, butter, and salt well. Give the mixture five minutes to settle.
2. Knead for roughly 3 minutes with damp hands.
3. Roll the dough into four balls. Put each ball between two plastic bags and flatten it to a quarter of an inch using a pot cover.
4. Put the butter in a nonstick pan that is set on medium heat. Cook the Arepas for 3 minutes on each side, until they become a golden brown.

27. COLOMBIAN CHEESE AREPAS

Prep Time: 10 Mins

Cook Time: 15 Mins

Servings: 3

Ingredients

- 1 cup of Precooked cornmeal Harina
- 1 cup of grated mozzarella cheese
- 1 cup of warm water
- 1 tsp salt
- 1 tbsp softened butter
- 1 tbsp vegetable oil for cooking

Instructions

1. Combine the cornmeal, butter, water, and salt in a bowl.
2. Shape the mixture into a smooth ball.
3. Cover with a cloth and let aside for 10 minutes.
4. Make clementine-sized balls and use a tortilla press plate to flatten them.
5. You should have 6 (5 inch) diameter discs.
6. Place a layer of mozzarella cheese in the middle of one of your corn discs and top with another disc.
7. Press the edges inward and down to secure them. Ensure that all the edges are sealed so that the cheese does not spill out when cooking.
8. Fill the cast iron skillet with oil, then place it over medium-high heat.
9. Place the Arepa in a cast-iron skillet or heated pan.
10. Cook for approximately 3–4 minutes on each side on medium high.
11. Serve right now, and if you'd like, top with more butter.

28. BLACK BEAN & PLANTAIN AREPA SANDWICHES

Prep Time: 15 Mins

Cook Time: 15 Mins

Total Time: 30 Mins

Servings: 6

Ingredients

Arepas

- 6 large Arepas

Plantains

- 2 large peeled ripe and spotty plantains
- 1 tbsp oil

Black beans

- 1 (15-ounce) can slightly drained black beans
- ½ tsp ground cumin
- 1 Pinch sea salt

Guacamole

- 2 ripe avocados
- 2-3 tbsp lime juice
- ¼ tsp sea salt (plus more to taste)
- ¼ cup of diced onion
- 2 tbsp chopped cilantro

For serving (optional)

- Cabbage
- Cilantro
- Habanero Hot Sauce (or other hot sauce)

Instructions

1. Make your Arepas now if you haven't already; they take around 30 minutes (not counting prep time).

2. Set oven temperature to 400 F (209 C). Peel your plantains and cut them into ½-inch slices on a diagonal. Stir with oil on a parchment-lined baking sheet. Spread out evenly and bake for 15-20 minutes, until the edges are caramelized and golden. When the timer is almost up, toss to ensure uniform baking.

3. Meanwhile, warm the black beans (slightly drained) in a small saucepan over medium heat until they are hot and boiling. Add salt and cumin for seasoning, then mix well. Next, turn off the heat and leave it alone (cover to stay warm).

4. Finally, make the guacamole by pounding the avocado and adding the lime, salt, onion, and cilantro to a small mixing dish. Mix well, then taste and make any necessary flavor changes. Add extra salt for saltiness, lime for acidity, or onion for crunch. Put away.

5. It's your turn to serve. Cut a "pita pocket" or in half and serve your hot Arepas. Add the beans, plantains, guacamole, and any additional toppings you'd want, like cilantro, cabbage, or Habanero Hot Sauce!

6. Fresh is best. Keep leftovers separate from one another for up to three days in the refrigerator.

29. AREPAS SIN CARNE

Prep Time: 5 Mins

Cook Time: 45 Mins

Total Time: 50 Mins

Servings: 4

Ingredients

- 1 batch Arepa dough
- 1 packet shredded mozzarella (or plant-based alternative)
- 1 large avocado
- 1 tin chopped tomatoes
- 300 g onions (2 medium onions)
- 250 ml water
- 180 g plant-based mince
- 2 tbsp olive oil
- 2 tbsp Sofrito
- 2 tbsp fresh coriander (packed)
- 2 cloves garlic

- ½ tsp turmeric
- ½ tsp onion powder
- ½ tsp oregano
- ½ tsp cumin
- ½ tsp annatto powder
- ¼ tsp garlic powder
- Salt & Pepper to taste
- oil for frying

Instructions

1. Place the dry spices in a small dish with the diced onions.
2. Put the olive oil in a pan and set the heat to medium-low. Sauté the onions for 5 minutes, until they're transparent and with subtle grill marks. Whisk in the sofrito next.
3. Stir in the spices and minced meat until well combined. Next, add diced tomatoes with their juice.
4. After that, pour in the water, mix, and lower the heat to a gentle simmer. Add the coriander and freshly squeezed garlic. After ten minutes of cooking, remove from the fire.
5. Put your Arepas in the oven according to the directions on the package. You may cut your avocado into tiny strips while they cook. Once the Arepas have slightly cooled, cut them open in the middle with an extremely sharp knife. Consider them similar to pita pockets. Stuff them with cheese, thin avocado slices tossed with lemon or lime juice, and heated mince.
6. Now preheat a big pan over medium-low heat and add a layer of extra virgin olive oil. Fry each side gently until brown and crispy. It takes around 2–3 minutes to crisp each side.

30. VENEZUELAN BLACK BEAN AREPAS CON QUESO

Prep Time: 10 Mins

Cook Time: 15 Mins

Total Time: 25 Mins

Servings: 2

Ingredients

Arepas

- ⅔ cup of cornmeal
- Salt to taste
- ⅓ cup of vegetable broth
- ½ tsp onion powder
- 1 tsp oil

Filling

- ½ small white onion
- 1 tsp olive oil
- 1 cup of cooked or canned black beans
- ½ tsp ground cumin
- ½ tsp dried thyme

Dip

- ½ small avocado (or ⅓ large avocado)
- 1 big handful finely chopped fresh parsley
- 1 tsp lemon juice
- 2 Ounces low fat crumbled feta cheese
- cilantro/coriander, fresh (for serving)

Instructions

Arepas

1. Combine the cornmeal, salt, onion powder, and ¼ cup of heated vegetable broth in a medium-sized bowl and stir. Add some additional broth if the dough is too dry. You should have a soft, flexible, moist dough. Stir until thoroughly combined, then set aside to rest for ten minutes.

2. Split the dough in half, then shape each half into two circulars, roughly 1 cm (0.4 inch) thick Arepas.
3. Put 1 tsp oil and the Arepas in a big, nonstick pan and bring it up to high temperature. Cook for about 3–4 minutes on each side over high heat, then decrease the heat to low. Cook until they are browned on both sides.

Filling

4. Add the onion, chopped, to a nonstick skillet and lightly sprinkle with oil. Decrease heat to medium and cook until the onion is transparent.
5. Add salt, cumin, thyme, and beans. Cook for three minutes after mixing. Add black pepper to taste.

Dip

6. In the meantime, combine the avocado, parsley, lemon juice, ¼ cup of water, and ¼ tsp of salt in a bowl. Add a little additional water if needed, and mash until smooth.
7. Add black beans, green sauce, chopped feta, and cilantro leaves to the inside or outside of the Arepas.

31. VEGAN AREPAS

Prep Time: 15 Mins

Cook Time: 25 Mins

Total Time: 40 Mins

Servings: 8

Ingredients

- 2 cups of pre-cooked cornmeal masarepa, white or yellow
- 2 tsp kosher salt
- 1 tbsp olive oil
- 2 cups of warm water, you may not need all

Fillings:

- vegan butter, black beans, shredded vegan cheese, curtido, slaw, pulled jackfruit, etc.

Instructions

1. Set oven temperature to 350°F.
2. Combine the salt and cornmeal in a large mixing bowl. Add the water gradually while continuing to whisk or mix with your hands. Add just enough water to make a soft, moist, but not sticky dough. Cover and let aside for 8-10 minutes, or until the liquid has been absorbed.
3. Divide dough into 8 balls, then roll each into a smooth disk approximately 2 ½ inches in diameter. Add extra water if necessary to avoid cracking.
4. After that, warm oil over medium heat in a large skillet. Add as many Arepas as possible while they are hot, leaving approximately an inch between each one. Cook for 2-3 minutes on each side, until it's golden brown. Move the Arepas that have browned to a baking sheet. Continue with the remaining Arepas.
5. Bake for 15-17 minutes, until the center is firm and the exterior is crisp.
6. Serve hot, with fillings or butter. Cut each Arepa in half, then stuff it with your preferred filling.

Notes

1. **To store:** Keep leftover Arepas in an airtight jar in the fridge for 3–5 days. They may be reheated in a pan over medium heat with some oil, or in an air fryer.
2. **To freeze:** They can be frozen for up to two months. Put them in an airtight container with layers of parchment paper between them. Thaw them in the fridge before reheating them in an air fryer or skillet.

32. VEGAN VENEZUELAN AREPAS

Prep Time: 20 Mins

Cook Time: 1 Hr

Total Time: 1 Hr 20 Mins

Servings: 6

Ingredients

For Jackfruit filling

- 1 (20 Ounces) can of jackfruit
- 2 tbsp oil
- 1 small finely chopped onion
- 2-3 finely minced garlic cloves

- 1 medium roasted and finely chopped poblano chili
- 1½ cups of low sodium vegetable broth
- 1 bay leaf
- ¼ cup of chopped cilantro
- To taste Salt & Pepper

For Black Bean Filling

- 2 tsp oil
- 1 small finely chopped onion
- 1-2 finely minced garlic cloves
- 1 medium finely chopped tomato
- 2 cups of cooked black beans
- ½ tsp ground cumin
- ½ tsp chili powder
- ½-1 cup of water
- To taste salt & pepper

For Venezuelan Arepas

- 2 cups of Venezuelan or Colombian style masa harina flour
- ½ tsp salt
- 2-2½ cups of warm water, more if needed
- As needed oil, for cooking the Arepa

Instructions

Make the Jackfruit Filling

1. Wash the jackfruit well, let it drain, and then use a fork to break the pieces into strands.
2. Add the shredded jackfruit to a heavy-bottomed pan with 1 tbsp of oil. Cook until it turns brown, turning often. Transfer to a plate.
3. After that, add the onion and garlic to the same skillet, heat the extra tbsp of oil, and sauté until the edges begin to brown.
4. Stir in the vegetable stock and roasted poblano, scraping along the sides to remove any brown pieces.
5. Return the pan with the browned jackfruit and bay leaf. Boil the mixture, then reduce to low heat and cook for around 15-20 minutes.
6. The jackfruit will be soft and have absorbed all of the flavors.

Make Black Bean Filling

7. Add the onion and garlic to heated oil in a saucepan and sauté until the scallions become translucent.
8. Add the tomato and simmer for approximately 2 minutes, until it gets mushy.
9. Add the water, salt, pepper, cumin, and red chili powder to the black beans and stir. Mix thoroughly and cook for 5-8 minutes, until it's thick and delicious.

Make Arepas

10. Add salt to a large bowl and mix in the precooked cornmeal.
11. make a hole in the center and fill with warm water to produce a soft dough. Any lumps can be removed using your fingertips. Make sure the dough is nice and, smooth and soft. If the dough looks too firm, add extra water.
12. Pinch out six equal pieces of dough, then roll each into a ball.
13. Gently massage the ball out on your hand to make it flat. It should result in a disc between 3.5" and 4" in width and 1" in thickness.
14. Place the 2-3 discs gently on a hot, lightly oiled pan. Cook on medium-high for 8-10 minutes until a crust form. After flipping gently, cook for another 8-10 minutes.
15. Now place Arepas on a baking sheet and bake for 12-15 minutes at 350° Fahrenheit, rotating them halfway through, or until cooked through and have a golden hue on both sides.
16. Slice and stuff these Arepas right away!

33. VEGAN MIXED MUSHROOM AREPAS

Prep Time: 15 Mins

Cook Time: 20 Mins

Total Time: 35 Mins

Servings: 4

Ingredients

Arepa cakes

- 2 cups of white cornmeal
- 1½ cups of warm water
- 1 tsp salt
- 1 tbsp olive oil (for cooking)

Mushroom mixture

- 8 Ounces sliced baby bella mushrooms
- 8 Ounces chopped oyster mushrooms
- 2 minced garlic cloves
- 1 tbsp taco seasoning
- 1 tbsp olive oil (for cooking)

Arepa fillings

- 4 Ounces vegan mozzarella cheese
- 4 Ounces guacamole

Instructions

1. To make a dough, combine the cornmeal, water, and salt in a large bowl. Give it five minutes to sit.
2. Prepare the mushrooms and garlic.
3. After that, add 1 tbsp olive oil to a large pan set over medium-high heat, then add sliced mushrooms. Cook the mushrooms until they are tender and turning brown, stirring often—about five minutes. Stir in the garlic after adding it. Cook for another minute, stirring regularly to avoid scorching the garlic. Stir the mushroom mixture for another two minutes after adding the taco seasoning: cover and reserve.
4. Shape the dough into little patties about ½-inch thick and 3–4 inches in diameter.

5. Next, heat one tbsp olive oil in a skillet or griddle over medium-high heat. Cook the Arepas in groups of three to four until they are browned all over—approximately 5 minutes per side. Proceed with the remaining cornmeal cakes after removing them from the pan.

6. Cut each Arepa ¾ of the way through to form a pouch using a serrated knife. Place a piece of vegan cheese, guacamole, and a tbsp of the mushroom mixture into each pocket. Serve right away and have fun!

34. AVOCADO PLUS CHICKPEA AREPAS

Prep Time: 1 Hr

Cook Time: 35 Mins

Total Time: 1 Hr 35 Mins

Servings: 6

Ingredients

For the Chickpeas and avocado

- 2 large roughly diced avocados
- 2 tbsp vegan mayonnaise
- 1 tbsp lime juice
- 1 (15-ounce) can drained and rinsed chickpeas
- ½ seeded and diced small red bell pepper
- ½ seeded and finely minced jalapeno
- 2-3 tbsp finely diced red onion
- 1 small finely minced garlic clove
- 3 tbsp finely chopped cilantro
- ½ tsp sea salt, or to taste
- Freshly Ground Black Pepper, to taste

For Arepas

- 2 cups of warm water
- 1 tsp salt
- 2 cups of corn flour
- ½ cup of additional warm water, if needed
- Vegetable Oil

Instructions

For the filling

1. Place the cubed avocado, lime juice, and vegan mayonnaise in a mixing bowl. Mix with a fork till the avocado is smooth and creamy. Mash the drained chickpeas with a fork. It's okay to leave some chickpeas whole; you simply want to tear them apart.
2. Add the remaining ingredients for the filling. Mix the ingredients gently—season with salt and pepper to taste. If necessary, increase the salt or lime juice.
3. Put in the refrigerator. Before using, let it cool down. I advise taking at least an hour to relax. It's better after a few hours.

For the Arepas

4. Combine the salt and the warm water in a large mixing bowl. Start adding the corn flour gradually. Use your hands to knead the dough until it comes together. You want the dough to be very wet. As necessary, add a little amount of the extra water if it starts to crack. Remove any lumps from the dough by pressing them out. Give the dough five minutes to rest.
5. Split the dough into six equal pieces. Form a ball out of each chunk of dough. Next, using the palms of your hands, shape the dough ball into a patty that is separated by 3-4 inches in diameter. Before creating the disks, moisten your hands with warm water if the dough is drying out and breaking during the rolling process.
6. Set the oven's temperature to 350°F. Wrap a baking sheet with parchment paper.
7. Warm a big skillet over medium heat with a little oil. Before adding the Arepa dough, let the pan to get hot. Transfer the prepared Arepas disks to the skillet in batches. Cook each Arepa for 4–6 minutes on each side until the light brown patches begin to appear. Transfer onto the baking sheet.
8. Cook the Arepas for 14-18 minutes on a baking sheet, flipping halfway through once they have all been cooked in the pan. They will be done cooking in the oven. Tap the completed portion with your hand and it will produce a hollow, firm sound. They should also be a lovely golden-brown hue. Take out of the oven.
9. Before handling, let it cool for a few minutes. Gently cut the Arepas in half, then stuff each half with the avocado and chickpea mixture. Serve right away!

35. VENEZUELAN AREPAS

Prep Time: 10 Mins

Cook Time: 10 Mins

Total Time: 20 Mins

Servings: 5

Ingredients

- 2 cups of masarepa harina
- ¾ tsp sea salt
- 2 cups of water

Instructions

1. Combine the masarepa flour and salt using your fingertips in a large mixing bowl.
2. Add water to a mixing bowl, then use your hands to combine the dough until no dry flour is visible thoroughly.
3. The masarepa will absorb water if you knead the dough for 3 minutes. Form a handful of dough into a ball and use your finger to make an impression to determine if the dough is excellent. It's important that the dough be pliable, soft, and doesn't break in the areas where you make the impression. Add some extra water to the dough if it cracks. Add a few tsp of water and knead until it becomes soft.
4. Prepare a dish or a flat surface for your made Arepa patties.
5. To prepare Arepa patties, form a chunk of dough between your palms into a ball about the size of a tennis ball. (For exact weight measurements per Arepa, refer to the notes.) Next, flatten the ball by gently pressing it a few times. To ensure uniform cooking, both surfaces of the Arepa should be as smooth as possible when in contact with the pan. Next, give the edges a little touch throughout. It's too dry if your Arepa dough breaks easily or crumbles as you try to form your patties. Re-add the dough to the bowl, mix in a little water, and knead everything together to include the water fully.
6. Transfer the molded Arepa patty to the plate and repeat the process with the remaining dough until it is used up.
7. Give your flat skillet a two-minute preheating period over medium-low heat. Make sure there is enough space in the pan for the Arepas to be flipped over by gently pushing them so they touch the bottom of the pan. Avoid packing the pan. If your skillet is wide, you may need to do this in batches.

8. Cook Arepas without moving for approximately five minutes. Next, carefully raise the first Arepa you added with a spatula to see if it is browning. If not, go on cooking while perhaps turning up the heat a little. Flip the Arepas and gently push them into the pan so they touch the heated pan's surface if the bottom of the Arepas is golden brown.
9. Cook for another 5 minutes on this end. When the Arepas have streaks of color ranging from golden to dark brown, the dough on the outside is crisp, and they feel quite solid when pressed. They need to be hot outside and soft and doughy in the middle.
10. Preheat your oven to 200°F. Put the Arepas on a baking sheet and bake them in the oven while you continue cooking them if you are making a big number and want to keep them warm while you make the rest.
11. Place the hot Arepas in a pot holder or a clean kitchen towel to fill them. Next, make an open pocket by cutting the Arepa ⅔ of the way through with a long, sharp knife. Place your preferred filling inside, then serve right away!

36. CHEESE-STUFFED AREPAS

Total Time: 50 Mins

Servings: 8

Ingredients

- Kosher salt
- 2 cups of pre-cooked white cornmeal
- 4 ounces of part-skim mozzarella, divided into 8 cubes
- ¼ cup of vegetable oil, or as needed

Directions

1. Preheat oven to 350° Fahrenheit and place a rack in the center.
2. Mix 1 ½ tsp salt and 2 ½ cup of lukewarm water in a large mixing bowl. Add the corn meal gradually to the water, stirring and combining with your fingertips until a soft and wet dough forms.
3. Split the dough into eight equal portions, roughly the size of golf balls, and shape each into a patty that is five inches in diameter and one-fourth of an inch thick.
4. Place a mozzarella cube in the middle of every burger. Make sure the cheese is well coated and sealed by folding the dough over it. Pat it down again until it is 3 inches broad and ½ inch thick.

5. Heat the oil in a large pan over medium-low heat until it shimmers. Cook the corn patties in batches, turning them over after 5 minutes on both sides until they are golden brown, being careful to keep the oil hot throughout. Bake for 10 minutes, till the edges are crisp and golden, on a cooling rack set on a rimmed baking sheet.

37. VEGAN COLOMBIAN AREPAS

Prep Time: 15 Mins

Cook Time: 15 Mins

Total Time: 30 Mins

Servings: 60

Ingredients

- 5½ cups of room temperature water
- 2 tsp salt
- 4 cups of pre-cooked yellow or white cornmeal
- 2-3 cups of shredded vegan mozzarella cheese
- ⅓ cup of nutritional yeast
- ¼ cup of vegan butter

Instructions

1. Combine the salt and water in a big bowl. Mix until the salt is dissolved.
2. Stir in vegan cheese, butter, nutritional yeast, and pre-cooked cornmeal. Mix thoroughly with clean hands or a wooden spoon until the dough is mixed and soft.
3. Use ½ cup of dough to make a bigger Arepa. Use ¼ cup of dough for a smaller Arepa. Form it into a ball, then use your hands to flatten it into a ½-inch thick layer. Repeat.
4. Put a nonstick pan or griddle over medium-high heat. Cook the Arepa for 5 minutes on each side in a hot, greased pan. Put it away and do it again. Add extra oil and lower heat as required. Serve and enjoy!

38. GLUTEN FREE STUFFED AREPA

Prep Time: 5 Mins

Cook Time: 6 Mins

Total Time: 11 Mins

Servings: 5

Ingredients

- 2 cups of cornmeal white
- 2 ½ cups of milk or water
- ½ tsp salt
- 2 cups of grated cheese shredded meat/fillings

Instructions

1. Pour the liquids, salt, and cornmeal into a bowl and stir.
2. Mix until a moist dough forms after adding all of the corn with a silicone spatula, spoon, or fingertips.
3. Set aside the dough for a few minutes to rest.
4. Grate the cheese and set it aside while the dough is resting.
5. Scoop some of the dough into your hands using your hands.
6. Roll into a ball and rotate it in the palm of your hand to cup of it and gently make a gap in the middle.
7. Add a small amount of cheese and secure with care.
8. Continue with the remaining dough after flattening the Arepa to a thickness of about ½ inch.
9. Now preheat a skillet over medium heat and lightly oil it with coconut oil when it is time to grill.
10. Grill the Arepas on all sides for 3-4 minutes, until they're golden.

Notes

1. Serve warm and enjoy! It could take a few batches to finish them all!

39. AREPAS WITH WILD-CAUGHT SEAFOOD

Prep Time: 5 Mins

Cook Time: 10 Mins

Total Time: 15 Mins

Servings: 4

Ingredients

- ½ cup of Arepa flour
- ½ cup of water
- Handful shredded cheese
- Sea salt, to taste
- Cooked seafood of choice
- High-heat cooking oil

Instructions

1. Mix the Arepa flour, water, salt, and cheese shreds together to form a dough that is wet. Flake any leftover fish into the mixture before producing the cakes.
2. Make a golf-ball-sized ball of dough, and then gently press it down between your hands to make a patty. Should the patty develop cracks on the edges, return the dough to the bowl and include additional water into the mixture. Add extra Arepa flour if the patty seems too wet. Form flat patties approximately 4-5 inches in diameter after the dough reaches the proper consistency. Continue with the leftover dough.
3. Warm some oil in a pan over medium-high heat until it foams. Fry the Arepas in the pan for 4-5 minutes on each side, until they become crispy and brown. Place a dollop of avocado, crème fresca, or butter on top of each Arepa, then heap it with fish.

40. AREPAS WITH SALMON AND SHRIMP

Servings: 4

Ingredients

- 4 Arepas, about 6"
- 3 cooked salmon fillets (5 ounces), sliced thinly
- 15 cooked and diced shrimp
- ¾ cup of mayonnaise
- 1 tbsp mustard
- 1 minced garlic clove
- ½ cup of chopped fresh cilantro, more for garnish
- ¼ cup of grated onion
- 1 lemon
- Salt and pepper
- ¼ tsp ground cumin

Instructions

1. Mix the mayonnaise, mustard, ground cumin, cilantro, garlic, and onion in a mixing bowl. Blend well.
2. Add the shrimp and salmon and fold. Add pepper and salt for seasoning.
3. Place an Arepa on a serving platter, top with the mixture, and garnish with cilantro.

41. GRILLED COBIA AREPAS

Prep Time: 30 Mins

Cook Time: 15 Mins

Total Time: 45 Mins

Servings: 4

Ingredients

For the fish

- Approx. 1.5 Pounds cobia fillets
- Kosher salt
- Freshly cracked black pepper
- 2 limes
- 2 minced garlic cloves

- 2 tbsp olive oil
- 1 tsp ground cumin
- 1 tsp smoked paprika

For the Arepas

- 2 avocados
- 1 lime
- 1 pinch of kosher salt
- 2 radishes, julienned
- ¼ head of shredded iceberg lettuce
- 1 sliced jalapeño
- 1 cup of crumbled queso fresco
- 1 big handful chopped cilantro
- 4 Arepas
- Hot sauce (optional)

Instructions

1. Place the fish fillets on a shallow dish or plate and pat them dry with a paper towel.
2. Pour the fish with a mixture of the juice from both limes, garlic, olive oil, cumin, and paprika. Flip the fish to coat it with the marinade. Set aside for 20 minutes to marinate.
3. In the meantime, prepare a gas or charcoal grill to medium-high and grease the grates.
4. Prepare your toppings as well:
5. After that, mash the avocado with a fork and season with salt and lime juice. Ready them for serving by chopping the remaining veggies.
6. Transfer the Arepas, fish, and marinade on the grill.
7. Brush the fish with the marinade and grill it until it's cooked through, turning it once. The fish should be ready in 6-10 minutes, based on its thickness.
8. Place the Arepas on the grill for about two minutes, until they are toasted and have some char marks.
9. Wait until the fish is cold enough to hand-cut.
10. Add the mashed avocado, fish, lettuce, radish, cheese, cilantro, and jalapeño to the Arepas. If preferred, add spicy sauce on top. Enjoy!

42. SHREDDED BEEF AREPAS

Prep Time: 30 Mins

Cook Time: 1 Hr 20 Mins

Total Time: 1 Hr 50 Mins

Servings: 8

Ingredients

For the shredded beef

- 2 tbsp avocado oil
- 2.5–3 pounds beef boneless chuck roast, cubed
- 1 sliced yellow onion
- 2 tsp chili powder
- 1 tsp salt
- 1 tsp garlic powder
- ½ tsp cumin
- ½ tsp oregano
- 2 bay leaves
- 16 ounces beef bone broth
- 16 ounces salsa
- 8 ounces mild green chiles

For the cilantro lime ranch

- 1 cup of cilantro
- 1 roughly chopped jalapeño, seeds removed
- 2 tbsp fresh dill
- 2 tbsp fresh chives
- ½ cup of avocado oil mayo
- ¾ cup of milk of choice
- juice of 1 lime
- ½ tsp garlic powder
- pinch of salt

For the Arepa

- 2½ cups of water
- 2 cups of white cornmeal

- 1 tsp salt
- 1 sliced avocado
- 1 cup of freshly grated raw cheddar cheese
- 1 cup of seasoned black beans, heated

Instructions

1. Select the Sauté option on the Instant Pot. Add the avocado oil when it's heated, then sear the chuck roast for ten minutes on each side. Add the remaining ingredients and thoroughly blend them together. Press cancel, secure the lid, and shut off the pressure valve before manually adjusting the pressure to high and holding the up button for thirty minutes. Remove the lid after 20 minutes of allowing the pressure to naturally discharge at the end of the allotted time.
2. Combine all ingredients for the cilantro lime ranch in a blender and process until smooth, while the beef is cooking. Refrigerate for the time being.
3. Start preparing the Arepa dough as soon as the instant pot's pressure releases. Fill a big bowl halfway with water, then carefully pour in the cornmeal, breaking it up with one hand and your fingers like a claw so it doesn't get clumpy. Add the salt once you've finished the last of the cornmeal. The mixture will make a fairly sticky dough. Give it a 5-minute break.
4. To cook the Arepas, you may use an ice cream scoop to obtain a slightly smaller amount, but I like to use a kitchen scale to ensure that all the dough balls are the same size (5–6 ounces). This will make around 7–8 dough balls. Press each ball into a patty shape with your hands. Cook for 5-7 minutes on each side on a nonstick pan over medium heat, till it begins to crisp and brown.
5. Transfer the beef and onions to a cutting board after removing them with a slotted utensil once the beef is done making. Using two forks, separate the meat. Put the meat and onions into a big, nonstick skillet. Scoop out about ½ cup of instant pot's liquid over medium-high heat and add it to the pan with the meat. Simmer for five minutes, until the liquid thickens and reduces.
6. Now all that is left for you to do is construct your Arepa by forming a pocket in the Arepa by cutting into it, but being careful not to cut all the way through it. Top with a dollop of meat, a few beans, a few avocado slices, some shredded cheddar cheese, and cilantro lime ranch sauce! Eat it!

43. BEEF AND BLACK BEAN AREPAS

Prep Time: 30 Mins

Total Time: 30 Mins

Servings: 10

Ingredients

- 3 cups of masarepa
- 1⅓ pound ground beef
- 2 onions
- 2 bell peppers
- 5 chiles
- 5 cloves garlic
- 1 tbsp cumin
- 1 tsp chili powder
- 3 tbsp chipotle hot sauce
- 1 can of black beans
- 8 Ounces queso blanco
- 1 can diced tomato

Instructions

1. Mix the Masarepa with the water according to the package guidelines. Each brand has a slightly different ratio. Tips for finding Masarepa: Examine the Mexican or Spanish cuisine. Make sure the product is labeled as Precocida or pre-cooked corn meal; there are several brands available.
2. Roll the dough into thin, ⅓-inch-thick circles. Cook over medium-high heat in a dry cast-iron pan until both sides are browned. Using a fork, split, preserving half of the edge to create a pocket.
3. Meanwhile, chop the garlic, chilies, onions, and peppers. If you don't want it as hot, remove the seeds from the chilies.
4. Drain most of the oil and brown the ground meat. Remove from the pan and put aside. Simmer the peppers and onions in a little oil. Salted. Add the garlic and chilies when they begin to brown. Coat everything by adding the cooked meat and stirring. Add the tomatoes and spicy sauce after that, then the seasonings. Add the rinsed beans. In order to really mix the flavors, simmer for fifteen minutes.
5. Place the crumbled queso on top of the meat and beans within the Arepas. Serve!

44. AREPA FILLED WITH SHREDDED BEEF & YELLOW CHEESE

Total Time: 2 Hrs

Servings: 12

Ingredients

- 10-12 Arepas with pre-cooked white cornmeal
- 2 pounds brisket
- mixed leafy greens
- 4 cups of water
- ½ cup of corn oil
- 1 large finely chopped onion
- 1 finely chopped red pepper; deveined, seedless
- 4 finely chopped ripe tomatoes
- 3 sweet finely chopped chili peppers
- 1 tsp Worcestershire sauce
- 1 tsp ground cumin
- 1 crushed garlic clove
- ½ cup of tomato paste
- salt and pepper to taste
- ½ pound shredded yellow cheese

Instructions

1. Cook beef for 30 minutes in a pressure cooker with green vegetables and water. Shred the meat finely, reserving a cup of the liquid. Put away.
2. Fry the pepper, tomato, onion, and sweet chili peppers in hot oil in same pot.
3. Add the tomato paste, Worcestershire sauce, cumin, garlic, broth, and salt and pepper to taste.
4. Add the shredded meat. Simmer on low heat for 20 minutes until the liquid is gone.
5. Place shredded meat and yellow cheese into each Arepa.

45. BEEF AND AVOCADO AREPA

Prep Time: 30 Mins

Cook Time: 40 Mins

Total Time: 1 Hr 10 Mins

Servings: 8

Ingredients

Arepa

- 2 cups of cornmeal
- 2 - 2½ cups of lukewarm water
- 2 tsp salt
- 2 tbsp melted and cooled butter
- 1 cup of shredded sharp cheddar cheese
- 4-5 tbsp avocado oil

Meat

- 1½ pounds ground beef
- ½ tsp salt
- 1 tsp onion powder
- 1 tbsp dried minced onions
- 1 tbsp beef Better Than Bouillon
- 1 cup of water
- ½ tsp cumin
- 1 tsp chili powder
- 1½ - 2 cups of shredded Mexican Blend cheese

Garnish

- Lettuce
- Avocado
- taco sauce

Instructions

1. Combine the butter, salt, cornmeal, and warm water. Once everything is well incorporated, knead it for a few minutes to make it smooth. While the meat is cooking, let it rest.

2. Brown the ground beef with salt, onion powder, and dried onions in a skillet. Remove any extra fat before adding Better Than Bouillon, water, cumin, and chili powder. Then simmer for 15-20 minutes on medium to low heat. Take the mixture off the stove and gradually add the cheese, stirring often, until it melts completely and the sauce thickens. Fry your Arepas and keep warm over low heat.
3. In a cast iron pan, heat a tsp or two of oil over medium heat. While the beef is cooking, keep it on low heat. Form the Arepa dough into spheres, flatten them into ½-inch-thick discs, and transfer them onto a heated pan. Fry for 6–7 minutes on each side, until it's cooked through and golden brown. Repeat with remaining dough, then transfer to a paper towel.
4. Fill the Arepas with beef and garnish with avocado, cilantro, and taco sauce once they have cooled to the touch. Slice the Arepas in the middle. Enjoy hot!

46. AREMPAS PABELLÓN AREPA

Total Time: 5 Hrs

Servings: 6

Ingredients

Shredded Beef

- 1 chuck roast, about 2 pounds
- 3 green onions
- 2 garlic cloves
- ½ cup of Sofrito (see recipe below)
- 2 tbsp sazon
- 1 tbsp garlic powder
- 1 tbsp Italian seasoning
- 1 tbsp paprika
- 1 tbsp salt
- Half a bunch cilantro

Dough

- 1 bag of precooked yellow cornmeal
- Vegetable oil, for cooking

Plantain

- Vegetable oil, for frying
- 1 Yellow Plantain

Beans

- 2 cups of cooked beans
- ¼ cup of Sofrito (see recipe below)
- 1 tbsp garlic powder
- 1 tbsp Italian seasoning
- 1 tbsp sazon
- 1 tbsp salt
- Quarter of a bunch cilantro
- Shredded mozzarella cheese for serving

Sofrito

- 1 bunch green onions
- 7 garlic cloves
- Half a yellow onion
- Half a red bell pepper, seeded and stemmed
- 2 tbsp vegetable oil

Directions

1. **For the Shredded Beef:** Dice the steak into little bits. Add to a big pot with the garlic and green onions. Make sure the meat is submerged in water. Boil, then reduce heat to a high simmer for three hours until the meat is cooked. (If necessary, add extra water.)
2. Remove the meat from the heat, drain, and save 1 cup of cooking liquid; discard the green onion and garlic. Return the steak to the pot after shredding it. Stir in the Sofrito (recipe follows), sazon, paprika, garlic powder, Italian seasoning, salt, cilantro, and the one cup of cooking liquid that was set aside. Then simmer over medium heat for ten minutes to evaporate most of the liquid. Put the steak away.
3. **For the Plantains:** Pour enough oil into a big pot to come halfway up the side. Preheat to 350 degrees Fahrenheit and attach a deep fat fry thermometer. Peel the plantain and cut on the diagonal into slices that are ½ inch thick. Fry in batches for approximately three minutes, until golden brown, flipping as required. Place on a paper-towel-lined plate using a slotted spoon.

4. **For the Beans:** Put the beans in a big pan over medium heat along with the sofrito (recipe below), garlic powder, Italian seasoning, sazon, salt, and cilantro. Stir and cook for around 6 minutes, until the flavors combine and the beans are heated.
5. **For the Dough:** Prepare enough dough for six Arepas by following the directions on the precooked cornmeal bag.
6. Take a piece of dough that is large enough to fit in your hand and roll it into a ball to form the Arepas. Start to make it flat, about the size and shape of a hamburger ball.
7. Fill a big pan with just enough oil to cover the bottom—heat on medium-high. Fill the skillet with as many Arepas as you can fit without packing it full. Simmer for 5 minutes on each side until it's browned. If necessary, repeat.
8. **Build the Arepas:** Gently cut open a pocket in an Arepa by inserting a tiny, sharp knife into its edge. Add chopped meat, plantains, beans, and cheese to the top of the shell after it has been opened. Proceed with the leftover ingredients. Enjoy after a large portion! This will be a messy but delicious dish.
9. **Sofrito**
   Yield: Makes about 1 cup.
10. Finely cut the pepper, yellow onion, garlic, and green onions. In a large pan set over medium-high heat, heat the oil. Add the vegetable mixture and simmer, stirring, until the onion is translucent and tender. Refrigerate and cool for up to three days.

47. BRAISED BRISKET STUFFED AREPA

Servings: 6

Ingredients

- 2 minced garlic cloves
- ¼ cup of Worcestershire sauce
- 2 tbsp white vinegar
- 1 finely chopped and divided white onion
- 4 tbsp olive oil, divided
- 18 ounces beef brisket
- 3 small chopped tomatoes
- 1 small chopped red pepper
- ½ tbsp cumin
- 1 small can of diced tomatoes
- 6 warmed Arepas
- Salt and pepper
- 9 ounces grated white Cheddar cheese

Directions

1. Mix the garlic, vinegar, Worcestershire sauce, half of the onion, and half of the olive oil in a mixing bowl to make a marinade—season with salt and pepper.
2. Place the beef brisket in a bag that can be sealed again and add marinade.
3. Close the bag, and for two hours, rub the marinade into the meat.
4. Set oven temperature to 300°F or 150°C.
5. Transfer the marinated beef and marinade to a roasting pan, then add sufficient water to cover the meat.
6. Cook for two hours or until the flesh pulls apart with a fork.
7. Warm remaining olive oil in a large cast-iron skillet over medium-high heat.
8. When the onions soften, add the remaining onion, fresh tomatoes, and red pepper and simmer for three to four minutes.
9. Add the cumin and cook, stirring frequently, for another minute.
10. Cook for five minutes after adding the canned tomatoes, and then stir in the cooked, shredded meat.
11. Add the salt and pepper, cook the beef for 2 minutes or until it's hot, and then take it off the stove.
12. Split the steak among the Arepas.
13. Add cheddar cheese on top. Serve hot.

48. VENEZUELAN SHREDDED BEEF AREPAS WITH CARNE MECHADA

Prep Time: 15 Mins

Cook Time: 2 Hrs 30 Mins

Total Time: 2 Hrs 45 Mins

Servings: 4

Ingredients

- 1.5-2-pound flank steak
- 1 onion sliced
- 1-tab cooking oil

Sauce

- 2 cups of beef broth
- 2 cups of water
- ½ tea black pepper

- ½ tea salt
- tomato diced
- 8-ounce tomato sauce
- 1 diced red bell pepper
- 1 diced yellow onion
- 1-tab Mexican oregano
- 3 minced garlic cloves
- 1-tab Worcestershire sauce
- 1 tea cumin
- 1 diced jalapeno

Instructions

1. Divide the flank steak into four halves. Warm up the oil on the mid-high seat. Brown the flank steak in the oil before adding the onion.
2. After that, add enough water to just cover the meat after adding the two cups of water and the two cups of beef broth.
3. Cover and simmer for two hours after bringing to a boil–then reducing to a simmer. Take out the meat and shred it from the beef broth. Keep the cooking liquid aside.
4. In a large sauté pan with high sides, heat the oil over medium heat. Incorporate the garlic, peppers, and onion. Tenderize the onions by sautéing them for 4–5 minutes.
5. Add the Worcestershire sauce, diced tomatoes, tomato sauce, cumin, oregano, and salt. Blend well. Stir in 2 cups of the saved beef stock along with the shredded meat. Heat the mixture until it boils. Simmer for 20 minutes, uncovered, on low heat.
6. As directed on the packaging, prepare the Arepas. Cook the Arepas in a heavy-bottomed pan or on a hot grill over direct fire until they are cooked through and have a lovely brown top and bottom.
7. Divide the Arepas in half and stuff with carne macheda.

49. GRILLED BEEF AREPA

Prep Time: 15 Mins

Cook Time: 20 Mins

Total Time: 35 Mins

Servings: 6

Ingredients

- 2½ cups of lukewarm water for the Arepas
- 1 tsp salt, for the Arepas
- 2 cups of precooked white corn meal for the Arepas
- 500 grams beef
- salt
- pepper
- fresh white cheese, sliced
- 2 sliced tomatoes
- 1 sliced avocado

Instructions

1. **For the Arepas:** Mix the salt with the lukewarm water in a bowl. Add the Precooked White Corn. Gradually add the flour and knead for two minutes until the dough is smooth. Give it a five-minute sit.
2. Make eight or ten equal portions of dough, then roll each into a ball. Roll each ball into a 4-inch round Arepas with your hands.
3. Cook Arepas for 5 minutes on each side until they're cooked through on a hot griddle set over medium heat. Slice the Arepas in half lengthwise and reserve.
4. **For the grilled beef:** Cook the meat on a grill or skillet to the desired doneness. Slice the grilled meat, season with salt and pepper, and reserve.
5. **For assembling the grilled beef Arepas:** Stuff Arepas with grilled meat, tomato, avocado, and queso fresco. Present the grilled beef Arepas beside guasacaca.

50. EASY AREPAS RECIPE

Prep Time: 10 Mins

Cook Time: 20 Mins

Total Time: 30 Mins

Servings: 8

Ingredients

- 2½ cups of lukewarm water
- 1 tsp salt
- 2 cups of corn flour
- 1 tbsp olive oil

Directions

1. Preheat oven to 350°F and wrap baking sheet with parchment or silpat.
2. Transfer the water to a medium-sized mixing bowl. When the salt is added, whisk it in until it dissolves.
3. To make a dough, add the corn flour to the water and mix with a spoon or your hands. Give the dough a five-minute rest.
4. Roll the dough into balls and use your hands to flatten them into Arepas patties that are approximately ½ inch thick and 3–4 inches in diameter.
5. In a big skillet or cast-iron pan, preheat the olive oil over medium heat. Place the patties on and cook for 3–4 minutes on each side, until they have caramelized.
6. Now place Arepas on a baking sheet and bake for 10 minutes.
7. Take out the Arepas and warmly serve.

51. AREPA WITH SHREDDED MEAT

Servings: 4

Ingredients

- 4 Arepas corn cakes, cooked
- 1 Carne Desmechada shredded meat recipe
- 1 tbsp butter
- 1 large peeled and diced ripe plantain
- 1 diced avocado
- fresh cilantro for garnish

Instructions

1. Melt butter in a medium-sized pan and add the chopped plantains. Leave the plantains to brown for three minutes and then set them away.
2. Place an Arepa on a platter and top with the carne desmechada, avocado, and plantain.
3. Add some fresh cilantro, then proceed to serve.

THE END

Printed in Great Britain
by Amazon

37492615R00037